# NEW PERSPECTIVES

# The Berlin Wall

## R. G. GRANT

WAYLAND

First published in 1998 by
Wayland Publishers Ltd,
61 Western Road,
Hove,
East Sussex BN3 1JD

This book was prepared for Wayland Publishers Ltd
by Ruth Nason.

Series editor: Alex Woolf
Series design: Stonecastle Graphics
Book design: LNbooks, Houghton Regis, Bedfordshire

Find Wayland on the internet at:
http://www.wayland.co.uk

British Library Cataloguing in Publication Data
Grant, R.G.
    The Berlin Wall. – (New perspectives)
    1.Berlin Wall, Berlin, Germany, 1961-1989
    I.Title
    943.1'55'087

ISBN 0 7502 2167 4

Printed and bound in Italy by G. Canale & C.S.p.A., Turin

Cover photos: an East
German guard; celebrations
on top of the Berlin Wall,
10 November 1989.

Page 1: West Berliners
wave across the wall.

## Acknowledgements

The Author and Publishers thank the following for their permission
to reproduce photographs: Camera Press: cover (background), pages
1, 8, 13, 21, 22, 25, 27, 28, 32, 34, 35, 36, 37, 39, 41, 42, 43, 44t, 44b,
45, 46, 47, 48, 49, 50, 51, 53, 57; Getty Images: pages 5, 10, 11, 24; Ole
Steen Hansen: pages 3, 26, 29; Popperfoto: pages 16, 19t, 19b, 20b, 31;
Topham Picturepoint: cover (foreground), pages 6, 7, 9, 12, 14, 15, 17,
18, 20t, 23, 30, 38, 40, 52, 55, 59.

# CONTENTS

Building the Wall              4

The Iron Curtain              11

Wall of Death                 23

Living with the Wall          30

Breaching the Wall            37

The Collapse of Communism     45

Living without the Wall       52

Date List                     60

Glossary                      62

Resources                     63

Index                         63

'Attention! You are leaving West Berlin' claimed the notice in front of the Brandenburg Gate.

# BUILDING THE WALL

### A city at the heart of the Cold War

Soon after the end of the Second World War, the Cold War had begun. The two sides in the war were the communist Soviet Union, with its East European allies, and the USA, with its allies in Western Europe. There was no direct fighting between them, but there was great hostility.

To make sure that people could not cross between the Soviet bloc countries and the West, the communists had created an 'Iron Curtain' across the centre of Europe, with barbed wire, minefields and border guards wielding machine guns. Almost 200 kilometres from the curtain, deep inside communist East Germany (officially called the German Democratic Republic, or GDR), lay a divided city: Berlin.

The divided city of Berlin lay far to the east of the Iron Curtain (shown in grey on this map).

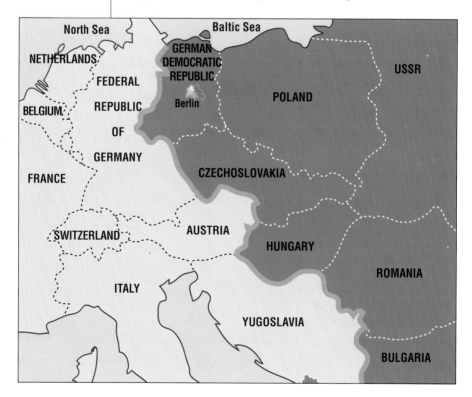

Berlin, July 1945: Troops of the British Victory Parade at the end of World War II rest under a picture of the British, American, and Soviet leaders; Churchill, Roosevelt, and Stalin. At the Yalta Conference in February 1945, these three had agreed to divide defeated Germany, and Berlin, into four zones.

East Berlin was occupied by troops of East Germany's ally, the Soviet Union. But West Berlin, more than half the city, was occupied by troops from the United States, Great Britain, and France. West Berlin was a small island of democracy lapped around by a sea of communism.

## Summer 1961

Under an agreement between the Soviet Union and the Western Allies, until August 1961 people had the right to move freely back and forth between East and West Berlin. For East Germans wanting to emigrate to Western Europe—a crime under East German law—Berlin presented a relatively easy escape route. As long as they did not attract the attention of the East German police (the Vopos), people could walk across the divide into West Berlin and from there be flown to a fresh life in West Germany (officially called the Federal Republic of Germany, or DDR).

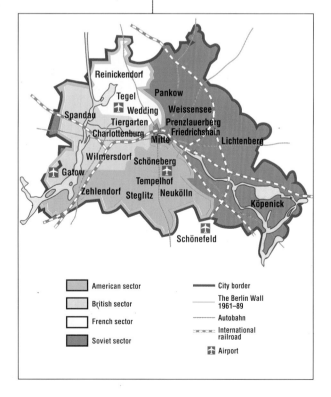

Berlin, 1945–1990

13 August 1961: East Berliners awoke to find barbed-wire barriers preventing them from crossing into West Berlin.

However, tension mounted in the city in the summer of 1961. The East German government had vowed to stop the flow of emigrants to the West, and the Soviet Union had threatened war if necessary to drive British, French and American troops out of West Berlin. Fearing that the last door open to the West was about to be closed, thousands of East Germans were fleeing to West Berlin every day. Many travelled from distant parts of East Germany, dodging the Vopos who were pulling people off trains and buses bound for East Berlin and turning back those whom they suspected of intending to emigrate.

On the hot night of Saturday, 12 - Sunday, 13 August, few Berliners slept easily in their beds. Tens of thousands of people in the East were making their final preparations to cross to the West in the following week. Families made elaborate plans to cross the border one at a time, in order to avoid attracting attention, and to meet up on the

## 66 'Measures against the slave trade ...'

The East German government called the Berlin Wall the Anti-Fascist Protection Wall. They claimed it was needed to stop the infiltration of Western spies and agents into the GDR. They also claimed that people were being unfairly seduced, or even forced, into emigrating to the West. Willy Stoph, the prime minister of the GDR, told the East German parliament:

'We are no longer prepared to sit back and watch the wooing away of huge numbers of the people of the GDR ... [The government must] take appropriate measures against the slave trade, the luring away of people, and against sabotage.' (Quoted in Tusa, *The Last Division*) 99

> ## Early call
>
> Daniel Schorr was head of the Berlin bureau of the American CBS broadcasting network in 1961. He was woken from his sleep on the night of 12-13 August:
>
> 'At 2.30 in the morning, I got a call from my cameraman. He said something very strange was going on at the sector border and that I should come down, so – grumbling – I got out of bed and went. Under floodlights and guarded by soldiers, engineering crews were using jackhammers to sink posts in the ground. Between the posts they were unrolling sheets of barbed wire. By 7 a.m., West Berliners were there, hooting and jeering.'
> (Quoted in *Newsweek*, November 1989)

other side. All knew that they might have been denounced by an informer to the feared secret police, the Staatssicherheitsdienst – or Stasi, for short. They had also all heard the rumour that the days of a free West Berlin were numbered.

## Dividing the city

At dead of night, trucks began to rumble through East Berlin. Packed with Vopos, Grepos (East German border police) and East German soldiers, they pulled up at points along the border between East and West Berlin. On the dark, deserted streets, they began to unload rolls of barbed wire and tools. At the Brandenburg Gate, in the centre of Berlin, a few Western police and soldiers watched helplessly as the East Germans drilled into the cobbles and tarmac to fix concrete posts. Next they strung barbed wire across to make a fence. By daybreak, a line of barbed wire and armed guards stretched for miles across the centre of the city.

14 August 1961: an East Berliner pleads vainly with Vopos to allow him to return home across the newly erected barrier.

17 August 1961: an East German soldier oversees work on building the wall, to make the barrier more permanent.

Unsure what was happening, crowds began to gather. Gradually, the certainty dawned: the communists were sealing off West Berlin. At the Brandenburg Gate there were clashes as West Berliners threw stones at East German guards and the Vopos responded with water cannon. All through that Sunday, people desperately sought a way through the as-yet incomplete barrier. Hundreds of East Berliners found the weak points in the new frontier and got across.

For example, in one place, the Teltow Canal formed the border between East and West. A family swam across, with a child strapped to its father's back. Another family crawled across the border through a cemetery left unbarred on that first day. Some people merely waited until guards were distracted, and sprinted across the wire. Everywhere, there was panic and confusion.

## Moving too late

Many people who were planning to move from East to West in the summer of 1961 were caught out by the speed of the closing of the border. One man, standing on the West Berlin side of the wall and looking eastward, told an American journalist his story:

'My wife's over there with our little boy. We lived over there, but we had to get out, so I rented a room over here and started bringing our things over a little at a time. They stayed there to cover up until the day we could all leave for good. Then it was too late.' (Quoted in *Time*, August 1961)

## Desperate to escape

Gradually, the loopholes were closed. Four days after sealing the border, the East Germans began to build a wall. Soldiers stood guard as building workers made breeze blocks into a barrier 2.4 metres high and topped with barbed wire.

Efforts to reach the West became more desperate. The border guards had orders to shoot to kill if necessary. On 24 August, Gunter Liftin became the first known victim killed trying to cross to the West. He died after being shot by border guards as he attempted to swim across the Teltow Canal.

Some of the most dramatic incidents occurred in Bernauerstrasse, where houses were right on the border line. If people stepped out of their front doors, they passed from the communist East to the West. The houses were evacuated and the ground-floor doors and windows on the Western side were sealed off but, at first, upstairs windows remained open. In the first weeks after the wall was built, Bernauerstrasse was repeatedly the scene of dramas, as people leaped from high windows into jumping sheets held out by the West Berlin fire brigade. Escapers even threw children down into the sheets and jumped from roofs in their desperation. Eventually all the windows were sealed with breeze blocks. The house fronts became the wall.

## Pain of separation

The line of the Berlin Wall divided the city crudely and irrationally. It separated communities, cut off customers from the shops they used, football fans from their team's ground, parishioners from their churches. It cut across bus, tram and rail routes. At only seven carefully controlled checkpoints were military personnel and foreigners with visas allowed to cross from West to East.

Bernauerstrasse, September 1961. As this woman tried to escape by jumping from an upstairs window, she was grabbed by East German soldiers. But a West Berliner climbed on to the lower windowsill and pulled her free.

## " Football deprivation

The wall disrupted the everyday lives of Berliners in a multitude of small ways. Many East Berliners were fans of the Hertha football club, whose ground was on the West side. Journalist Simon Kuper describes how a Hertha fan tried to cope with suddenly being cut off from the club:

'For the first few months after the Wall went up, he spent Saturday afternoons standing beside it among a mass of East Berlin Hertha fans, listening to the sounds coming from the Hertha ground just a few hundred yards from the frontier. When the crowd at the ground cheered, the group behind the Iron Curtain cheered too. Soon the border guards put a stop to this.' (From *Football Against the Enemy*)   "

May 1964: some West Berliners make the most of the wall, as a suntrap.

At a stroke, people lost jobs, friends, or lovers stranded on the other side of the wall. Thousands of families were split. Husbands could not contact their wives, or parents their children, caught on opposite sides of the divide. People stood on either side of the wall, holding up new-born babies to be seen by relatives, staring hopelessly in search of loved ones.

### Cold War symbol

The Berlin Wall immediately became the key symbol of the Cold War division of Europe. It made the issues seem very simple. On one side of the wall were democracy and prosperity; on the other were oppression and shortages. Desperate people were prepared to risk their lives to cross the wall to freedom. But the reality of the wall was never quite that straightforward. In some ways, its existence served the interests of the West as well as the East. And its eventual fall, in 1989, would create a host of new problems.

# THE IRON CURTAIN

The Second World War ended in 1945. Germany, ruled by Adolf Hitler and his Nazi Party, was totally defeated by an alliance led by the USA, the Soviet Union and Britain. In April 1945, American forces driving eastward met Soviet forces advancing westward at the River Elbe in Germany. Soviet troops fought their way into Berlin, and Hitler committed suicide amid the ruins of his capital.

Transport systems in Berlin, destroyed during the war, took a long while to repair. In 1946, people were still taken to hospital by hand ambulance.

## " Berlin in ruins

In 1945, at the end of the Second World War, Berlin had been devastated by bombing and shellfire. Willy Brandt, a future mayor of Berlin and German chancellor, described the ruined city in his memoirs:

'Craters, caves, mountains of rubble, debris-covered fields ... no fuel, no light, every little garden a graveyard and, above all this, like an immoveable cloud, the stink of putrefaction. In this no man's land lived human beings. Their life was a daily struggle for a handful of potatoes, a loaf of bread, a few lumps of coal, some cigarettes.' (*People and Politics*) "

## SOCIALISM AND COMMUNISM

The socialist movement began in the nineteenth century. Socialists felt that the world was being run by the rich at the expense of the poor. They blamed 'capitalism', the system under which industry, banks and land were owned by individual businessmen and investors, and run for maximum profit. They claimed that the capitalist 'free market' led to a society based on greed and injustice. Socialists believed that the state should run the economy, taking control at least of major industries and redistributing wealth from the rich to the poor.

In 1917, a revolution brought extreme socialists, the Bolsheviks, to power in Russia. They founded the Soviet Union, where industry, banks and land were owned by the state, and only one political party, the Communist Party, ran every aspect of society. The socialist movement across the world split between communists, who aligned themselves with the Soviet Union, and social democrats, like the British Labour Party, who wanted to bring about change through parliamentary democracy. The Soviet bloc states called the system in their countries 'socialist'. They thought of 'communism' as an ideal that would only be achieved some time in the future. But in the West, the Soviet bloc countries were always called 'communist'.

The communists saw themselves as involved in a struggle to overthrow 'capitalism', and to 'build socialism' in the countries under their control. In their eyes, capitalist societies were corrupt and decadent. They thought that socialism could prove more efficient than the free market and that the state would make the economy work for the benefit of all working people. They believed that the eventual collapse of capitalism and triumph of socialism were inevitable.

A cartoon from the official communist newspaper in Czechoslovakia, in 1949, shows Winston Churchill applauded by the rich, while workers (in the background) demonstrate against him.

The Americans, Soviets and British had discussed during the war what they would do when they had won. They had agreed to divide Germany into four zones. Each one of these zones would be occupied by one of the four most important Allies: the Soviet Union, the USA, Britain and France. Germany's capital city, Berlin, lay within the Soviet zone. But it was agreed that the capital would also be divided into four zones, or sectors. After Germany surrendered, the Allies put their plan into effect without a hitch. The Soviets allowed American, French and British troops to occupy their sectors of Berlin.

2 May 1945: a Soviet soldier hangs his country's flag from the Reichstag (parliament) building in Berlin.

The division of Germany and of Berlin was not intended to last. A joint Allied Control Council was set up to oversee all four zones. The Allies thought they would cooperate after the war, as they had during it. Eventually, it was assumed, a peace treaty with Germany would lead to the withdrawal of the occupying forces.

## The Allies fall out

But the wartime Allies quickly began to fall out. The Soviet Union was a very different country from Britain or the USA. It was ruled by the dictator Joseph Stalin and the Soviet Communist Party, which controlled every aspect of Soviet life. The communist state owned almost all factories, farms and shops. State propaganda services decided what people could know and what they should think. Anyone who criticized Stalin or communism in the slightest way might be arrested by the secret police and sent to a prison camp.

In defeating the Germans, Soviet troops had occupied all of Eastern Europe, including Poland, Hungary, Czechoslovakia, Romania and Bulgaria. They began to install governments in these countries modelled on that of the Soviet Union. Communist parties were given all real power. All other political groups were suppressed or forced into docile collaboration. Freedom of speech was not allowed and political police made arbitrary arrests. Czechoslovakia was the last Soviet-occupied country to fall under communist control, in early 1948.

## 66 Churchill and the Iron Curtain

Winston Churchill had been Britain's prime minister during the Second World War. In 1946, in a speech at Fulton, Missouri, Churchill tried to alert the USA to the risk of a Soviet takeover of Europe. He described the peoples of Soviet-controlled Eastern Europe as fatally cut off from the West:

'From Stettin on the Baltic to Trieste on the Adriatic, an iron curtain has descended over the continent.'

Although Churchill did not invent the phrase 'Iron Curtain', its widespread use to describe the border between Eastern and Western Europe dates from his Fulton speech. 99

The Western Allies, led by the USA, protested against these events in Eastern Europe. They believed that they had fought in the Second World War for democracy and freedom. Now, Eastern Europe was being subjected to governments that offered neither.

By 1947, US President Harry S. Truman had come to see the spread of Soviet-style communism as a worldwide threat to the interests of the USA. Western Europe looked especially vulnerable to a communist takeover. There were strong Soviet-backed communist parties in many West European states. Also, the Soviet army was by far the most powerful in Europe, and might be tempted to advance westward. Truman felt that the USA must act to stop Western Europe falling under communist domination. He provided millions of dollars for a European Recovery Programme, known as the Marshall Plan, to rebuild West European economies ruined by the war. This aid from the USA weakened support for the anti-American communist parties.

Give a free way to the Marshall Plan, said this West German poster.

## " Choosing East Germany

After the end of the Second World War, a considerable number of Germans freely chose to live in East Germany rather than the West. One reason was the relationship between West Germany and the Nazi past. Many top civil servants and industrialists in West Germany had played prominent roles in Nazi Germany. Some people, especially of Jewish origin, preferred East Germany because it was clearly run by people who had opposed the Nazis.

Another reason for choosing East Germany was an idealistic belief in socialism. The German novelist Stefan Heym, for example, returned from the USA to East Germany in 1952, inspired by the belief that socialism was creating a more just world, free of inequality. Heym told an interviewer in the 1980s:

'I believe that socialism is the form of human society that carries the future. And though a lot of things that have happened in socialism were tragic, very stupid and very bloody, I still am of that mind.'

Heym was, however, outspokenly critical of many actions of the East German communist government. His works were censored, he was spied on by the Stasi, and at one point he was put under house arrest. "

As hostility grew between the Soviet Union and the Western Allies, the situation in Germany became tense. Britain, France and the USA wanted to begin rebuilding the German economy from the ruins of the war. They also wanted to create a democratic German government. The three zones of Germany controlled by the Western Allies included more than two-thirds of Germany's population and most of its heavy industry. Despairing of reaching an agreement with the Soviets, in February 1948 the Western Allies began to plan setting up a German government in their zones alone. The Soviet Union was deeply hostile to this plan.

In June 1948, a new Deutschmark was introduced in the three zones of Germany occupied by Britain, France and the USA. This currency reform provoked an immediate response from the Soviet Union. The Soviets cut off access to Berlin by road and rail. The city was 190 kilometres inside the Soviet zone of occupation. The Soviets believed that the Western Allies would either have to withdraw from their sectors of Berlin or abandon the currency reform.

Supplies of food are unloaded from American army planes at Tempelhof airport, Berlin, June 1948.

## The Berlin blockade

There were 2.5 million people in the Western-occupied sectors of Berlin. They were already living on meagre rations, in a city still in ruins from wartime bombing. It seemed that, under blockade from the Soviet forces, the population must starve. However, led by their mayor, Ernst Reuter, the people of West Berlin were defiant. They called on the Western Allies to back them in resisting a communist takeover.

The Soviet Union had not cut off access to West Berlin by air. With little hope of success, the British and Americans embarked on an airlift of food and fuel. It was estimated that 4,500 tonnes of supplies a day would be needed to keep West Berlin's population alive. A standard transport aircraft at that time could carry only 3 tonnes. The pilots had three narrow air corridors to fly through to get to Berlin. The aircraft had to stay within these corridors, or Soviet fighters would have had an excuse to attack them.

The unloading of planes was organized so efficiently that the pilots and air crew had only a few minutes for a cup of tea before they took off again.

## The all-night airlift

A US soldier, Sergeant Cloyde Pinson, was posted to the US airbase at Bremerhaven, in northern Germany, during the Berlin airlift. He later remembered his first impressions on arriving at the base in the middle of the night:

'Planes were taking off every 30 seconds, soldiers were loading trucks, the maintenance shops were a beehive of activity, and the mess halls and clubs were open. It was a 24-hour operation ... The commanding officer stood in the control tower with his stop watch, checking the timing of the planes ... To most, it seemed an impossible task to meet all the needs of more than 2 million people by airlift. But except for water, Berlin was supplied with everything by the airlift.' (Quoted in Heins, *The Wall Falls*)

## ❝ No more slavery

Ernst Reuter, a Social Democrat, was elected mayor of Berlin in 1946. He rallied Berliners in resistance to the Soviet blockade. On 24 June 1948, Reuter urged a Berlin crowd to refuse the dictatorship of the Communist Party, which he likened to Hitler's Nazis:

'With all the means at our disposal we shall fight those who want to turn us into slaves and helots of a party. We have lived under such slavery in the days of Adolf Hitler. We want no return to such times ...' ❞

Miraculously, by August 1948, the airlift had reached the tonnage needed to guarantee survival. Flights continued throughout the worst winter weather, at the cost of 54 airmen's lives. Berliners had a poor diet and only four hours' electricity a day, but they came through. In May 1949, the Soviet Union admitted defeat and lifted the blockade of West Berlin.

Children had a day off school to celebrate the end of the blockade.

## ❝ Under blockade

Thasillo Borchart was a child living in Berlin during the blockade. Almost 50 years later, he told an interviewer:

'I remember vividly those twin-engined American planes dropping supplies, while hundreds of Germans applauded and waved, hardly able to believe that those same planes had been the enemy just four years earlier ... I was 10 years old. I asked my mother why all the American potatoes were so uniformly round and big. I had never seen big potatoes like that before ...'
(Quoted in Heins, *The Wall Falls*) ❞

## Germany divided

In the same month, the Federal Republic of Germany, or West Germany, was set up in the British, French and American occupation zones. The following October, the Soviet Union turned its zone into the German Democratic Republic (GDR), or East Germany, under a communist government. Both West and East Germany gained full formal independence in 1955.

In West Germany, a Christian Democrat, Konrad Adenauer, was elected chancellor. Rapid economic growth soon made the country one of the most wealthy in Europe. This was the 'German economic miracle'. East Germany, however, was weakened as the Soviet Union plundered goods and equipment to rebuild its own war-shattered economy. The communist East German government, dominated by Walter Ulbricht, poured all its resources into state-controlled heavy industry. As West Germans began to enjoy a new prosperity and cheap consumer goods, the East Germans were asked to work hard for little reward, under the watchful eye of the Stasi.

Dr Konrad Adenauer, chancellor of the new Federal Republic of Germany.

Members of East German workers' militias march through East Berlin. By joining militia units in their factories, these part-time soldiers made a show of support for the communist regime.

Demonstrators from East Berlin in June 1953 march through the Brandenburg Gate carrying West German black, red and gold flags.

In June 1953, resentment broke out into open revolt. Workers were ordered to work harder for longer hours, with no increase in wages. In East Berlin and elsewhere in East Germany, they went on strike. Faced with mass demonstrations calling for democracy and union with West Germany, the East German government called for Soviet support. Soviet tanks moved on to the streets of East Berlin and crushed the uprising.

The Western powers did nothing to help the revolt in East Germany. Three years later, in 1956, they also stood by while Soviet tanks crushed an uprising against communist rule in Hungary.

The funeral ceremony for seven of the victims of the Berlin uprising. More than 70,000 Berliners attended.

A member of the hated State Security Police is hung from a tree during the Hungarian uprising, November 1956. The uprising was soon ended by the arrival of Soviet tanks.

The USA and its allies tacitly accepted Soviet domination of Eastern Europe, because it could not be challenged without fighting a massively destructive war.

## Commuters and spies

By the mid-1950s, the situation of Berlin was an extraordinary one. The Soviets recognized East Berlin as the capital of East Germany, while the Western Allies considered West Berlin to be part of West Germany. But the city continued to be occupied by the troops of the four wartime Allies. Officially, East Berlin was just the Soviet-occupied sector, and West Berlin was the British, French and American sectors.

## A poetic solution

Bertolt Brecht was a famous German poet and playwright. After the Second World War, he chose to live in East Germany, because he believed in communism. But he became increasingly disillusioned with the East German government. After the June 1953 uprising in Berlin, the East German Writers' Union criticized the German people for failing to support communism. It said that the uprising had made the communist government lose confidence in the people. Brecht wrote a satirical answer to this in a poem called 'The Solution':

'Would it not then
be simpler for the government
to dissolve the people
and elect another?'
(Quoted in Ash, *The Uses of Adversity*)

George Blake worked for British Intelligence, but had secretly become a communist in the 1950s. In 1961 he was sentenced to forty-two years in prison for passing secrets to the Soviets. He escaped in 1966 and took refuge in the Soviet Union.

About 60,000 people who lived in communist East Berlin actually worked in West Berlin, commuting across every day. East Berliners crossed to the West in the evenings to go to the movies. British and American army officers stationed in West Berlin sometimes went to the opera in East Berlin.

Berlin became a centre for every form of spying and underhand conflict between East and West. It has been estimated that 12,000 people in Berlin earned their living by spying in the late 1950s. Spies moved in both directions across the open border. Stasi agents raided West Berlin to kidnap enemies of the communist government. The British and American intelligence agencies dug a huge tunnel stretching under East Berlin to intercept Soviet telephone calls, although this was betrayed to the Soviets by a British double agent, George Blake.

Neither side in the Cold War was happy with the situation in Berlin. The Soviets would have liked to take over West Berlin. The Western Allies were keenly aware that they could not defend West Berlin if it was attacked. Yet they were totally committed to staying there. This made the city a potential flashpoint that could have set off a nuclear war.

## " Warsaw Cafe

A former intelligence agent described the Warsaw Cafe, a notorious centre for espionage activity in the Soviet sector of Berlin in the 1950s:

'A sort of Stock Exchange for secrets, with half the tables taken up by Soviet, Czech, Polish, British, American, French, and East and West German agents. The going rate for a scrap of negotiable information could fall as low as five pounds. A few dollars were enough to make many of the boys change sides between cups of coffee.' (Quoted in Cookridge, *George Blake, Double Agent*) "

# WALL OF DEATH

Once the Iron Curtain had cut off communist-ruled Eastern Europe, Berlin was the only place where East Germans could find an easy route to a new life in the West. In the 1950s, about a quarter of a million East Germans emigrated each year by crossing into West Berlin. There they were housed at a refugee centre until room could be found on an aircraft to fly them out to West Germany.

There was no mystery why East Germans chose to emigrate. The West could offer them far higher wages and better living conditions, as well as basic freedoms such as the right to travel abroad and to express their own opinions. West Germany represented hope.

The East German border guards, who had to stop people crossing the Berlin Wall, were normally young conscripts. They had not volunteered for the job and often did it reluctantly.

### 'I couldn't take that any more'

Many East Germans' main reason for emigrating to the West was to improve their standard of living. But another major reason was to escape the atmosphere of distrust and fear created by the East German secret police. In August 1961, an East German who had crossed to start a new life in the West described the atmosphere in the East to an American journalist:

'The police no longer drag people out of their houses in the middle of the night. But the agents are still everywhere. You sit in a movie house watching a film, and suddenly the lights go on and you wait while the Vopos walk down the aisle looking everyone over. You wonder who they are after. When they motion to someone to get up and go with them, you relax. But the next time it could be you ... I couldn't take that any more.' (*Time*, August 1961)

Most of those who left East Germany were young and had valuable skills. The effect of their emigration on the East German economy was devastating. In the decade up to 1960, around one in seven of the entire East German population emigrated. This left East Germany short of plumbers, electricians, doctors, engineers, and almost every other kind of skilled or educated worker.

The East German communist leaders knew that if emigration continued at this level, their state would soon collapse. In March 1961, Ulbricht won backing from the Soviet Union for a plan to build a wall across the centre of Berlin, if all other solutions failed. The race to emigrate became more intense as rumours spread that the door to the West through Berlin might be slammed shut. Over the Easter weekend in 1961, 3,000 East German emigrants crossed into West Berlin in four days. By July, 30,000 a month were deserting the communist state.

The Soviet leader Nikita Khrushchev on a tour of France, 1960.

## Cold War crisis

Meanwhile, Berlin had become the focus of an intense Cold War crisis. The USA had a new president, John F. Kennedy. The Soviet leader, Nikita Khrushchev, thought Kennedy might be bullied into

## Ulbricht's denial

At a press conference on 16 June 1961, the East German communist leader Walter Ulbricht told reporters:

'The construction workers of our capital are for the most part busy building apartment houses, and their working capacities are fully employed to that end. Nobody intends to put up a wall.'

However, the decision to fence off West Berlin had secretly already been taken.

## " American encouragement

In the summer of 1961, many leading American and British politicians hoped that the communists would find some way of stopping the flow of refugees through Berlin, while leaving West Berlin free. In July, US Senator William Fulbright, the head of the Senate Foreign Relations Committee, said on American television:

'I don't understand why the East Germans don't close their border, because I think they have a right to close it.' (Quoted in Tusa, *The Last Division*) "

concessions over Berlin. At a summit meeting of the two leaders at Vienna in June 1961, Khrushchev demanded the withdrawal of Western forces from Berlin in six months and the absorption of West Berlin into East Germany. If this did not happen, he implied, there might be war.

The prospect of war between the USA and the Soviet Union was an almost unimaginable horror. Both countries had growing arsenals of nuclear weapons – bombs and missiles so powerful that a single one could destroy an entire city. A nuclear war would certainly kill tens of millions of people, and might destroy most life on earth through deadly radiation.

Yet Kennedy took Khrushchev seriously. He made a speech stating that the USA would resist any attempt at a communist takeover of West Berlin. The Americans began to build shelters, in preparation for a possible nuclear war.

John F. Kennedy, the new US president, attends a reception in Vienna given by the president of Austria.

❝

## A sense of relief

Theodore Sorensen was an adviser to President Kennedy. He recalled how the news of the building of the Berlin Wall was received:

'I was in the president's office at the White House just after he heard the news … It's hard to describe anything as outrageous or immoral as the Wall as bringing about a sense of relief, but compared to military alternatives or the continuing destabilization of the area, the Wall was better. We were afraid Khrushchev would carry out his threat of halting access to West Berlin.' (Quoted in *Newsweek*, November 1989)

❞

On 13 August 1961, when American leaders learned that the East Germans were sealing off West Berlin to stop emigration, they were on the whole relieved. It meant the crisis might be resolved without a war. The Allied forces in West Berlin were all prepared to resist a Soviet attack or a blockade. They had no plans to react to the building of a wall, and so did nothing. Privately, many Western leaders felt that sealing the border was a good solution to the Berlin problem. They also welcomed the Berlin Wall as a great opportunity for propaganda, since it showed the communists in such a bad light.

### Berlin betrayed

The failure of the Western Allies to respond to the building of the Berlin Wall was bitterly criticized by Berliners, including West Berlin's mayor Willy Brandt. But the only time the USA worked up a confrontation over the issue was in October 1961, when East German border guards refused to let some US officers go to the theatre in East Berlin unless they showed their passports. This minor diplomatic incident led to a stand-off between American and Soviet tanks across the checkpoint known as Checkpoint Charlie.

Checkpoint Charlie, 1979.

Foreign political leaders came to both sides of the wall to gaze and to pass comment. Khrushchev came to East Berlin and called the wall a 'great and heroic socialist achievement' – although in private he considered it ugly. Kennedy came to West Berlin and spoke in praise of freedom. But, basically, the wall satisfied both sides in the Cold War. After the building of the wall, Berlin ceased to be a possible flashpoint for world war. With its population safely imprisoned behind the wall, East Germany would survive. And West Berlin could continue to exist as an island in the communist sea.

President Kennedy at the Brandenburg Gate, 1963. The East German authorities had covered the arches with red cloth to prevent him from seeing into East Berlin and to prevent East Berliners from seeing him. On Kennedy's left is Willy Brandt.

## 66 'Ich bin ein Berliner ...'

In June 1963, President Kennedy visited West Berlin and made a famous speech from the balcony of the city hall. He declared:

'There are many people in the world who really don't understand, or say they don't, what is the great issue between the free world and the communist world. Let them come to Berlin. There are some who say communism is the wave of the future. Let them come to Berlin ... All free men, wherever they may live, are citizens of Berlin, and, therefore, as a free man, I take pride in the words "Ich bin ein Berliner" [I am a Berliner].'

The cynical inhabitants of West Berlin, who remembered Kennedy's lack of action when the wall was put up, claimed that the president had said he was a doughnut – since a 'Berliner' is also a jam-filled pastry. 99

It was left to the local people to cope with the painful realities of the wall. For two years all communication between East and West Berlin was cut off, even by telephone or letter. Tens of thousands of families – husbands and wives, parents and children – had been separated by the wall and were trapped on opposite sides with no news of or contact with one another. This went on until Christmas 1963, when West Berliners were allowed to queue to cross the wall for a brief visit to relatives in the East. Other small concessions followed, but did little to alleviate the pain of separation felt by so many.

## Running the wall

Thousands still tried to cross the barrier. The original 2.4-metre-high breeze-block wall was far from impassable. But the death rate among those who tried to 'run' the wall was high. The most infamous incident occurred on 17 August 1962, when 18-year-old Peter Fechter was shot by border guards as he tried to climb the wall. He was left lying at the foot of the wall for an hour until he bled to death.

There were many others: Paul Schultz was shot dead as he tried to cross on Christmas Day, 1963; 18-year-old Marienetta Jiskowski, three months pregnant, was shot eight times; Siegfried Noffke, who dug a tunnel under the wall to let his wife and child join him in West Berlin, was shot by East German guards as he emerged into East Berlin. In all, 86 people are known to have died trying to cross the Berlin Wall.

There were always successes to encourage more escape attempts, however. For example, in December 1961 an East German train driver took

East German police lift the body of Peter Fechter, who was shot down while trying to cross the wall in 1962.

24 relatives and friends on board his commuter train and drove it safely into West Berlin. A tunnel, dug from East to West under Bernauerstrasse, allowed 57 people to escape in two days, before it was discovered by the East German authorities. Another tunnel, started in an East Berlin graveyard, was the escape route for about 150 men, women and children.

Looking across the wall from West to East Berlin, 1979.

Through the 1960s, the wall was 'improved' and strengthened. By the end of the decade, the original rather flimsy structure had been replaced by a concrete wall 4.9 metres tall. Behind it was a 91-metre-wide 'death strip', floodlit at night, patrolled by dogs, and overlooked by watchtowers. An electrified fence at the East Berlin edge of the strip completed this formidable barrier. The wall certainly looked as if it was there to stay.

Gradually, the number of attempts to go under, over or through the wall dwindled. It had achieved what had been intended – to stop mass emigration from East Germany. But in the process it had revealed to the whole world that communist East Germany could only survive by making its people prisoners of the state.

# LIVING WITH THE WALL

In 1969, the former mayor of Berlin, Willy Brandt, was elected chancellor of West Germany. The following year he made a historic visit to East Germany, the first by a West German leader. Brandt saw cultivating better relations with East Germany and the Soviet Union as the only way forward for his country.

In 1971, Erich Honecker became effective leader of East Germany. Although Honecker had masterminded the building of the Berlin Wall in 1961, under the orders of Walter Ulbricht, he was more open than his predecessors to improving relations with the West. In 1972, East and West Germany accepted one another's existence as separate states, and both joined the United Nations.

## Brandt's policy

West German chancellor from 1969 to 1974, Willy Brandt believed that the Berlin Wall could only come down if the Cold War between East and West ended. He therefore worked for better relations with East Germany and other countries in the Soviet bloc. In his memoirs, he wrote:

'The power confrontation between East and West has ... overshadowed the German situation and divided Europe. We cannot simply undo this division. But we can endeavour to alleviate the results of this division and to contribute energetically to a process that begins to fill up the trenches that separate us in Germany.'
(*People and Politics*)

For Berliners, the practical effects of better relations between the two Germanies were considerable. Telephone links between East and West Berlin were restored, and West Berliners were allowed to visit East Berlin whenever they wished, after buying a one-day visa at one of the checkpoints in the wall. Like real-life Cinderellas, they had to be sure they arrived back in West Berlin by midnight. Almost all East Berliners, however, were still banned from visiting the West.

At the opening session of the eighth Congress of the Socialist Unity Party of East Germany, 1971. Erich Honecker is on the right. On the left is Willy Stoph. In the centre is Leonid Brezhnev, Secretary General of the Central Committee of the Communist Party of the Soviet Union.

## Life in East Germany

According to the communist leaders of East Germany, the East German people were building a socialist society based on equality. This society was morally superior to the capitalist West, with its emphasis on competition and its exploitation of workers by the rich. But, in reality, East German society was far from equal. Members of the ruling party and their families enjoyed valuable privileges, from education at the best schools to occupying the most prestigious apartments.

To a degree, life in East Germany improved in the 1970s. Wages rose and working hours fell. More people had fridges and television sets – on which they watched West German programmes.

The East German team at the opening ceremony of the Olympic Games in Moscow, 1980.

There was less persecution of non-communists. After years of harassment by the authorities, the Christian churches were at last allowed to operate freely. There were political prisoners, but, in general, as one German journalist put it, in East Germany 'the rules are clear, and as long as you stick to them, nothing will happen to you'.

It is reckoned that about one in ten East Germans more or less sincerely supported the communist regime. The rest were mostly resigned to their lot. Rents were low, food and transport were cheap, and jobs were secure. People concentrated on conquering the difficulties of everyday life, such as obtaining a Trabant car – for which there were long waiting lists. Many developed a certain patriotic feeling for their state, especially when East German athletes began to do well in the Olympic Games. Among themselves, East Germans grumbled about the shortcomings of their country, but if West Germans were present, they often defended it against criticism.

## Short supply

Shortages of many items such as fresh fruit or coffee were a constant fact of life in East Berlin. After the wall came down, one woman recalled:

'Nobody left the house in the morning without a string bag in her purse – just in case she heard of fresh groceries available somewhere in town. You might for instance hear on the train to work that a load of fresh oranges had just been delivered to a certain store at the other end of the town. You had to decide between being on time to work ... or being an hour or two late in order to get secure a week's supply of oranges. I still have the habit of buying too much and hoarding it. I can't get used to the idea that I can always get what I want.' (Quoted in Heins, *The Wall Falls*)

66

## Communist inefficiency

In the 1980s, journalist John Ardagh claimed that most people found life in East Germany 'perfectly liveable', but that the average East German citizen was annoyed by many things:

'If he were asked what annoys him most, he would probably put first the ban on travel to the West, and he might then add the distortions, omissions, and tedious repetitiveness of the State newspapers and media, which he can compare nightly with Western TV. But more likely he would cite ... the unpredictable shortages in the shops and the difficulties in getting the simplest repairs done. "If communism were less plain inefficient, people would accept it much more easily", said one housewife.' (*Germany and the Germans*)

99

But East Germany remained a very unfree society. All political and economic life was dominated by the communist Socialist Unity Party. Political slogans decorated the streets. Factories and farms were run by the state, and so were the trade unions that supposedly represented the people who worked in them. Workers were forced to hold meetings in their lunch breaks to declare their support for the struggle for communism in countries such as Cuba and Vietnam.

66

## Socialist hell

Jokes were one of the main ways East Germans expressed their disgruntlement with their society. For example:

'Question: "When you die, would you rather go to a capitalist hell or a socialist hell?" Answer: "A socialist hell, of course. You get roasted in the flames of hell in both cases; but in a socialist hell, there is a shortage of matches, they've run out of wood, and the Devil is not working at the moment."' (Quoted in Fulbrook, *Anatomy of a Dictatorship*)

99

When the Czechs tried to liberalize their regime in 1968, Soviet troops were sent in to stop such a move. The Soviets dropped propaganda leaflets in the streets of Prague, but the Czechs defiantly burned them.

All young people were heavily pressured to join the communist youth organization, Free German Youth, which tried to teach them communist values rather than the 'corrupt' individualist ideas of the West. Only selected people considered 'reliable' were allowed to travel outside the Soviet bloc.

### Secret police

Everyone knew that agents and informers for the secret police, the Stasi, were everywhere. The Stasi had 85,000 employees and over 170,000 regular informers. It kept secret files on more than one in three of the population. Stasi talent-spotters even operated in schools, targeting children who could be groomed for use as spies. When they finished their education, they would be found specific jobs – for example, as army officers or university professors – and would spy on their colleagues. Many informers were more casual, simply agreeing to occasional chats with Stasi agents. Everyone knew that to make progress in your career or get a good flat, you needed to show you were an enthusiastic and loyal communist. This often meant informing on your friends.

A steady trickle of people still tried to cross illegally to the West, usually by paying professionals who specialized in arranging border crossings. Many of

66          **Voting farce**

One of the few ways people in East Germany could protest against the communist regime was by refusing to vote in the communist-run elections, in which no opposition candidates were allowed to stand. British author Timothy Garton Ash observed that many working-class people in a poor area of East Berlin, Prenzlauer Berg, refused to vote:

'The remarkable abstention rate in ... Prenzlauer Berg reflects a long tradition of protest and a certain unbroken working-class pride. "Why should I take part in a farce?" as one building worker put it.'
(*The Uses of Adversity*)          99

these professionals were common criminals. They bribed guards and produced false documents. Mostly, people were carried across the border in the boots of cars. Often the professionals were in league with the Stasi and betrayed escapers. Those caught trying to escape were put in prison, and then sold to West Germany by the East German authorities. Selling political prisoners was a regular source of hard currency for the GDR.

An increasing number of people were allowed to go to the West after applying for visas through official channels.

## Challenging communist power

Throughout the 1970s, the division of Europe between the communist East and the liberal democratic West seemed an unshakeable fact of life. Communists had a virtually unchallenged hold on the Soviet Union, defied only by a handful of dissidents such as Alexander Solzhenitsyn and Andrei Sakharov who had almost no popular support. And the power of the Soviet army guaranteed the grip of communist regimes on the rest of Eastern Europe.

Prague, 1968: defying a Soviet tank sent in to restore tight communist control.

The Czech communists, led by Alexander Dubcek, had attempted to liberalize their regime in 1968. The period was called the 'Prague Spring'. Censorship was lifted and this brought an outpouring of fresh ideas and popular enthusiasm. But in August 1968, the Soviet Union, backed by its East European allies including East Germany, invaded Czechoslovakia to restore hardline communism. Soviet tanks on the streets of Prague spelled out a clear message to all of Eastern Europe: the people must accept communist government as there to stay.

Lech Walesa, leader of the Polish Solidarity movement.

Pope John Paul II visits his Polish homeland in 1987. The pope put all his authority behind the struggle to free Poland from communist rule.

The first crack in the solid mass of the Soviet bloc came in Poland. The Poles had always been potentially the most rebellious people in Eastern Europe. They had a fierce nationalism and hated the Soviet domination of their country. Also, their deep attachment to Roman Catholicism protected them from communist indoctrination. Twice, in 1956 and 1970, strikes and riots forced Polish communist leaders to resign, only to be replaced by other communist leaders who promised reforms that came to little.

The election of a Polish pope, John Paul II, in 1978 carried Polish national and religious enthusiasm to new heights. In 1980, an independent trade union movement called Solidarity was founded in the shipyards of the Polish port of Gdansk. Led by an electrician, Lech Walesa, Solidarity organized a strike that forced the communist regime to concede significant freedoms.

The following year, there was a clamp-down. With the backing of the Soviet Union, Polish army leader General Jaruzelski imposed martial law and arrested Solidarity activists. Yet the communists had lost face. People began to believe that communist rule might not last for ever.

# BREACHING THE WALL

At the beginning of the 1960s, the leader of the Soviet Union, Nikita Khrushchev, said confidently that socialism would 'bury capitalism'. He believed that one day the state-run economies of the Soviet bloc would overtake the economies of the West. But, by the 1980s, illusions about economic progress in the Soviet bloc had been shattered. Although official figures partly disguised what was happening, communist leaders knew that their economies were in deep trouble. Throughout the Soviet bloc, roads and housing were in disrepair, machinery was outdated and inefficient, and many factories produced little except pollution. Hampered by cumbersome bureaucracies and lacking the drive provided by free enterprise, the countries of the East were falling ever further behind the West in technology and living standards.

Mikhail Gorbachev, General Secretary of the Communist Party of the Soviet Union, 1985-91.

In 1985, Mikhail Gorbachev became leader of the Soviet Union. He was determined to reform the Soviet system and make communism work efficiently. He declared two watchwords: glasnost, which meant greater freedom of information, freedom of speech, and partially free elections; and perestroika, which meant changes to make the economy better organized. He was also determined to end the Cold War, which was forcing the Soviet Union to spend massive sums on weapons that it could not afford. Gorbachev intended to save Soviet communism, not to end it. But his reforms soon unleashed forces he could not control. Given freedom of speech, the Soviet people soon revealed that they were far more critical of communism than their rulers had supposed.

Above all, the changes implemented failed to improve the Soviet economy. Instead, they led to widespread disruption and a sharp fall in output. By 1989, the Soviet Union was seething with discontent.

## The Sinatra Doctrine

The changes in the Soviet Union were a serious threat to the rulers of communist Eastern Europe. The basic law of political life in Eastern Europe had been the Brezhnev Doctrine, named after the 1970s Soviet leader Leonid Brezhnev. It laid down that the Soviet Union and its allies would intervene by force to stop any East European country deserting communism. But in 1989 Soviet spokesman Gennady Gerasimov announced that the Brezhnev Doctrine had been replaced by the Sinatra Doctrine – a reference to Frank Sinatra's hit song 'I Did It My Way'. In other words, the East European countries were to be allowed to choose any form of government they liked, without interference from the Soviet Union.

In Poland and Hungary, the communists were ready to bow to the tide of change. The Polish government had privately accepted since 1980 that Lech Walesa's Solidarity movement had genuine widespread support. Solidarity proved its strength again with a series of crippling strikes in 1988. The following year, Solidarity was legalized and triumphed in elections. In August, the communists renounced their hold on power and a non-communist, Tadeusz Mazowiecki, became prime minister.

In Hungary, which had for long been the most liberal East European country, non-communist political parties were allowed to organize from the start of 1989 and reforms progressed rapidly. In May 1989,

Celebrating the end of communist control in Budapest, Hungary, October 1989. The flag with the communist symbol cut out from the middle was a symbol of the 1956 Hungarian uprising.

Lech Walesa campaigning for Solidarity in the elections of 1989.

some sections of the barbed wire fence that marked the Iron Curtain between Hungary and Austria were removed. Although no one knew it, this simple gesture was the beginning of the end for communist East Germany and the Berlin Wall.

## Hardliners cling on

The East German communist leaders, like their counterparts in Czechoslovakia, were appalled by Gorbachev's reforms and struggled to resist change. The spectacle of these elderly leaders carrying on as if nothing was happening while the whole communist world was plunged in turmoil finally disillusioned many of the East German people. Denied hope, they once more turned to mass emigration.

### " Rejecting change

The East German communists at first refused to follow the example of the reforms brought in by Gorbachev in the Soviet Union. In 1987, an East German spokesman, Kurt Hager, used an image from everyday life to make the point:

'You don't need to change the wallpaper in your flat just because your neighbour is redecorating his place.' "

**''** 'The Wall will remain'

By 1989, many East German leaders were completely out of touch with reality. At the start of the year, the head of state, Erich Honecker, was still convinced that he could hold on to power. Asked if the Berlin Wall was likely to come down, Honecker stated:

'The Wall will remain as long as the reasons for its presence have not been eliminated. It will still be there in 50 or even 100 years.'
(Quoted in McAdams, *Germany Divided*)     **''**

East Germans were generally allowed to travel to other Soviet bloc countries such as Poland, Czechoslovakia and Hungary. When they learned that Hungary's border with Austria was weakening, it started an avalanche. Through the summer of 1989, thousands of East Germans set off for Hungary, evading checks by the Stasi. Eventually the Hungarians gave up the effort to keep the border with Austria closed and tens of thousands of East Germans moved across it.

West German embassies in Poland and Czechoslovakia were also besieged by East Germans demanding to be taken to the West. In 1989 one and a half million people applied for official permission to emigrate – one in ten of the East German population. In all, 200,000 emigrated in the first eight months of that year.

For the first time, an opposition movement was organized inside East Germany. The Neues Forum group were mostly earnest young people who wanted to see East Germany develop some form of socialist democracy. They were protected from the Stasi by the

An East German crosses into Austria, September 1989.

churches, which had won a certain immunity from the operations of the secret police. The churches allowed them to hold meetings and organize protests from church property, which the Stasi would not enter to arrest them. Neues Forum demanded free elections, freedom of travel, and the abolition of the Stasi. Inspired by Neues Forum's example, thousands of East Germans began to join demonstrations on the streets, especially in the major city of Leipzig.

## Gorbachev in Berlin

In the middle of this crisis, in October 1989, the GDR celebrated its 40th anniversary. Communist leaders from around the world, including Gorbachev, were invited to East Berlin for the occasion. The Soviet Union had already decided that the only hope for saving communism in East Germany was to get rid of Honecker's hardline leadership. Soviet leaders had had talks with East German communists such as former espionage chief Markus Wolf, who would be prepared to lead a reform movement.

East German refugees arrive in the West from Prague, Czechoslovakia, and receive Red Cross help.

## 66 Well-fed refugees

In 1989, as East Germans fled the country in their thousands, many leading figures in East Germany still thought some aspects of their society were praiseworthy. Manfred Gerlach, a non-communist East German politician who supported the communist regime, expressed this view:

'Despite the problems, socialism has also brought many achievements to this country. We have social security, no unemployment, low inflation – this is the result of socialist development ... In the entire world, there are no better-fed or better-dressed refugees.' (Quoted in *The Guardian*, November 1989)

99

66

## Coming to terms

As East Germany collapsed, many sincere East German communists had to come to terms with the mistakes of the past. Salomea Genin was a woman who had voluntarily chosen to live in the GDR because of her communist beliefs. Disillusioned, she handed in her party card in early 1989. She told journalist Matthew Engels:

'I regret I took so long to see reality. I became a communist at a young age and became blind ... I have to admit I never thought about the shooting or the deaths. The wall was one of those things that were necessary for the upkeep of the system, and the system was the most important thing.'
(Quoted in *The Guardian*, October 1997)

99

When Gorbachev came to Berlin, he told Honecker there must be change, saying pointedly: 'He who is late will be punished by life itself.' To the East German people he said: 'If you want democracy then take it.'

Neues Forum demonstrators, November 1989.

On 9 October in Leipzig over 100,000 people demonstrated against the East German regime. The government planned to use the army and the police to halt this protest by force, but at the last minute the orders to do so were withdrawn. Even hardliners admitted at last that the pressure for reform was irresistible.

66

## A breath of fresh air

On 4 November 1989, author Stefan Heym addressed about half a million people who had gathered in Alexanderplatz, East Berlin, to demonstrate against the communist state. Heym expressed the relief that many felt:

'It's as if someone has thrown open a window after years of dullness and fug, platitudes, bureaucratic arbitrariness and blindness.'

On 18 October, Honecker was replaced by a more flexible communist, Egon Krenz. Krenz met representatives of Neues Forum, but progress towards reform was too slow. Across East Germany, thousands of communists were resigning their posts and tearing up their party cards. On 4 November, half a million people demonstrated in the centre of East Berlin. Bowing to the logic of events, Krenz planned to allow freedom of travel from 10 November. People would be issued exit visas on demand.

A communist official, Gunter Schabowski, gave a press conference on the evening of 9 November. He mentioned, in a casual and confused way, that people were now free to travel to the West. People began to wander towards the Berlin Wall, wondering whether this could possibly be true. Border guards with no clear instructions began to allow them through. At midnight, Krenz gave orders to open the border.

On the night of 9-10 November 1989, Berliners climbed on top of the Berlin Wall and began to attack it with hammers and chisels.

## Night of celebration

*Time* magazine described the ecstasy of Berliners when the wall opened on the night of 9-10 November:

'They tooted trumpets and danced on top. They brought out hammers and chisels and whacked away at the hated symbol of imprisonment, knocking loose chunks of concrete and waving them triumphantly before television cameras. They spilled out into the streets of West Berlin for a champagne-spraying, horn-honking bash that continued until past dawn and then another dawn.'

East Germans surged through the barriers, to be greeted by excited West Berliners. A massive street party began. Young people climbed on top of the wall in a demonstration of triumph. The division of the city was over.

Champagne-spraying, to celebrate the arrival of East Germans in the West, 10 November 1989.

## Free for the first time

Kristina Matschat was an East Berliner who joined the protest movement in the autumn of 1989. She described the night the wall opened:

'Strangers embraced, laughing, crying … Until three or four o'clock that morning, the Brandenburg Gate, the symbol of the German people, was open. Some people climbed onto the wall to dance. Suddenly we were seeing the West for the first time, the forbidden Berlin we had only seen on TV or heard about from friends. When we came home at dawn, I felt free for the first time in my life. I had never been happier.' (Quoted in Heins, *The Wall Falls*)

Fireworks and dancing.

# THE COLLAPSE OF COMMUNISM

In the week after the wall opened, about three million East Germans crossed into West Berlin. Given 100 Deutschmarks 'greeting money' to spend by the West Berlin authorities, they returned home laden with oranges and bananas, Walkmans and DIY equipment. Nonetheless, the wall was still an international border – people crossing were issued with exit visas – and the communists still ruled East Germany.

12 November 1989: parts of the Berlin Wall were removed by crane, to create border crossings.

But the momentum of the fall of communism in Eastern Europe was irresistible. In Czechoslovakia, mass demonstrations forced the communist government to resign on 24 November 1989 in the 'Velvet Revolution'. By the end of the year, author Vaclav Havel, the leader of the opposition to communist rule, was installed as the Czech president. In Romania, the communist dictator Nicolae Ceausescu and his wife Elena were executed by firing squad on Christmas Day.

Street sellers offered pieces
of the Berlin Wall for sale
to tourists. Larger pieces
were sold at auction, for
up to $20,000 each.

In East Germany, on 6 December, Egon Krenz resigned and the country had its first non-communist head of state, Manfred Gerlach. Two weeks later, the communist Socialist Unity Party that had ruled East Germany for 40 years changed its name to the Democratic Socialist Party. Headed by Gregor Gysi, it promised to adhere to freedom and democracy. Former East German leaders, including the Stasi chief Erich Mielke, were put under arrest.

A torrent of revelations about the communist regime caused outrage in East Germany. People were shocked to discover that the communist leaders had allowed themselves luxuries, such as villas with swimming pools, while preaching equality. In mid-January 1990, demonstrators stormed the headquarters of the Stasi in Berlin. They found 175 kilometres of secret files on over six million of the country's inhabitants. Every East German had known about the Stasi, but the discovery of the extent of their spying was devastating.

## Lies and humiliation

In the months after the wall opened, there were many revelations about the lifestyles of the former communist rulers and corruption in the communist state. These revelations had a powerful impact on East Germans. Kristina Pagels, who was a teenager at the time, remembers:

'We felt above all that we had been lied to. It was humiliating. Of course, we had been cynical about the endless propaganda. Yet, despite ourselves, we had still been taken in. We had not guessed the half of it. People felt angry and bitter – perhaps angry at themselves, as well. I had been a member of the FDJ [the communist youth organization]. I did it because everyone did. Now I was ashamed.' (From an interview with the author)

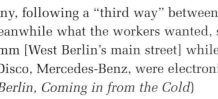

### Workers and intellectuals

Ken Smith is a British writer who was living in Berlin in 1989. He described the split that opened up, after the wall came down, between ordinary East Germans and the idealistic intellectuals who had led opposition to communism:

'What the thinkers wanted was a reformed GDR, socialist and democratic, the other Germany, following a "third way" between capitalism and communism. Meanwhile what the workers wanted, sauntering down the glittering Ku'damm [West Berlin's main street] while the lights flashed Schmuck, Sex, Disco, Mercedes-Benz, were electronics, oranges, Western fruit.' (*Berlin, Coming in from the Cold*)

### Uniting Germany

Immediately after the Berlin Wall opened, West German chancellor Helmut Kohl spoke of the possible reunification of the two Germanies. However, opinion polls showed that, in mid-December 1989, seven out of ten East Germans were opposed to reunification.

The idea was also opposed by the four victors of the Second World War, Britain, the USA, France and the Soviet Union. The Western Allies, whose troops still officially controlled West Berlin, feared that any suggestion of unifying Germany might frighten the Soviet Union and make it reverse its policy of accepting the fall of communism in Eastern Europe. There were still over 300,000 Soviet troops stationed in East Germany.

Russian troops stayed in eastern Germany until 1994. The German government paid the cost of resettling them in Russia.

## " Against reunification

The Neues Forum movement, which had organized opposition to the communist regime in East Germany in 1989, campaigned against German reunification. Neues Forum wanted East Germany to follow a democratic socialist 'third way' between communism and capitalism. The movement quickly lost popular support. In 1990, a Neues Forum leader commented:

'Of course we feel betrayed. We were out there demonstrating, risking arrest or even being shot, and now we are shouted down for suggesting that quick unification might not be the best solution. People imagine that it will be the answer to all their dreams, but of course it won't.' (Quoted in Ardagh, *Germany and the Germans*) "

However, enthusiasm for reunification grew rapidly. The opening of the wall did not end the crisis that had brought down the communist regime in East Germany. Emigration to the West continued. Above all, the East German economy faced open competition from the West. It was immediately obvious that most of East German industry could not survive, as cheaper and better Western consumer goods flooded the shops. By January 1990, the mass of East Germans felt their only chance for economic survival lay in unification with West Germany.

July 1990: the day before the East German currency was replaced by the West German Deutschmark, people hurried to buy petrol at cheap East German prices.

East Germany's first and last democratic elections were held in March 1990. They were dominated by the West German political parties, which set up branches in the East. Neues Forum and other East German opposition groups simply had no organization to win votes. The elections were a clear victory for Helmut Kohl's Christian Democrats, with 48 per cent of the vote. The only East German party with a significant following was the former communist party, which won almost one in six votes.

On 1 July, as a preparation for unification, the East German currency, the Ostmark, was replaced by the West German Deutschmark. East Germans were allowed to change their Ostmarks for Deutschmarks on a one-for-one basis. This was a massive windfall for East Germans who had savings, because their Ostmarks were really worth only a fraction of the powerful Deutschmark. Most people now consider that the one-for-one exchange rate was a disastrous measure, which destroyed at a stroke the only trump card East German industry held: its cheapness.

East Germans on their first day of shopping with Deutschmarks, July 1990.

A series of discussions on German reunification, known as the 'four-plus-two' talks, were held between Britain, the USA, France and the Soviet Union – the four – and West and East Germany – the two. The Soviet Union agreed to allow Germany to become united and, if it wanted, to join the Western alliance. In return, West Germany agreed to pay the Soviets about 12 thousand million Deutschmarks. On 12 September, a 'Treaty of the Final Settlement with regard to Germany' was signed in Moscow. It was, in effect, a belated official ending of the Second World War.

On 3 October 1990 Germany became a unified nation again. The celebrations were not as enthusiastic as they had been almost a year earlier when the Berlin Wall had opened. It was clear that, in reality, East Germany was being taken over by West Germany. East Germans already realized that the fall of the wall and reunification were far from an end of their problems.

## The fall of the Soviet Union

As Germany came together, the Soviet Union was falling apart. Gorbachev's gamble on reforming communism had failed totally. He had believed that, given a measure of freedom and democracy, people would support communism. But Soviet political reforms were too hesitant and partial. The state-controlled economy of the Soviet Union could not be made efficient. And communism had too much blood on its hands from the bitter days of the past for people to support it now.

Celebrating reunification, in Berlin.

## Returning home

Many people who had left East Germany for the West years before went back to visit once the wall was open. Most found it a dispiriting experience. Margarethe Fuchs described going back to her husband's childhood home in the East:

'We walked up and down the street where he used to ride a bike and play. Like his old home, all the houses had been sorely neglected. Weeds grew out of the walls, balconies were missing, side staircases lay in rubble, paint peeled, leaves from years before rotted in the yard. Although it was a crisp January day with a clear blue sky, the street seemed grey and colourless ... We thought at least the house and the neighbourhood would look like we had remembered them. We had hoped that somebody had taken care of what we had left behind.' (Quoted in Heins, *The Wall Falls*)

## " Seizing the moment

Some West Germans felt that reunification should have happened faster and been more wholehearted. They saw it as a great opportunity for the East Germans, but one they might miss because of the habits of thought learned under communism. In 1991, West German politician Robert Vogel said:

'Reunification came not too early but a year too late. It shouldn't have taken place on 3 October 1990, but instead right away in the same year that the wall fell ... On that very special November night in 1989, people from the East and West fell into each other's arms. Germany should have been united there and then ... Now the question is, will people ... jump at the opportunity reunification offers, or will the socialist slovenliness continue to rule?' (Quoted in Heins, *The Wall Falls*) "

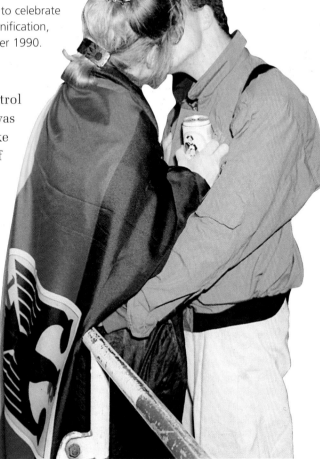

A kiss to celebrate German reunification, 3 October 1990.

In 1991, Gorbachev lost control of the Soviet Union. The economy was in steep decline and strikes broke out. The Soviet Union consisted of many national republics and their elected leaders began to pursue independence. In August 1991 an attempted coup by communist hardliners in Moscow failed dismally. Boris Yeltsin, the elected leader of the Russian Federation – the largest part of the Soviet Union – banned the Communist Party. By the end of 1991, all the Soviet republics had become independent. The Soviet Union ceased to exist and Gorbachev, its last leader, had no country to rule.

# LIVING WITHOUT THE WALL

The fall of communism aroused high hopes throughout Eastern Europe and the former Soviet Union. But the problems the new governments faced were immense. They had to create completely new political and economic systems based on a Western model. They had to cope with a legacy of factories producing goods that no one wanted to buy, with equipment that was decades out of date. Massive investment was needed in infrastructure such as roads and telephone lines.

In cities such as Warsaw, Prague and Moscow, the signs of economic progress were soon clearly visible, with consumer goods plentifully available and expensive Western cars on the streets. Yet for many people, the fall of communism brought poverty and insecurity. The cost of living rose rapidly. Unemployment levels shot up as uneconomic businesses and factories closed. In many places, basic services such as hospitals and public transport suffered as state spending and subsidies were cut. There was a great deal of crime.

Some parts of the former communist bloc were racked by warfare. In Georgia, Chechnya and Armenia many lives were lost. But the most extreme breakdown was in the former communist state of Yugoslavia. From 1991, Yugoslavia began to break up as the different nations within its borders pushed for independence. Croatia and Serbia came into conflict, but warfare really boiled over when multi-racial Bosnia declared independence. Serbs fought Croats and Muslims for domination of Bosnia, in a brutal war that cost an estimated 200,000 lives. Many people were massacred in acts of 'ethnic cleansing'.

Helmut Kohl is sworn in as chancellor of the newly united Germany, 17 January 1991.

Czechoslovakia was also split apart by nationalism in 1993, although without bloodshed. The Slovaks left the Czech Republic to set up their own state, Slovakia.

## Bitterness in Germany

In Germany, the fall of the Berlin Wall was followed by a honeymoon period during which East Germans were welcomed with open arms in West Germany. But the honeymoon soon came to an end. In the half century following the division of Germany in 1945, East and West Germans had had a very different experience of life and had become very different people. The Easterners, or 'Ossis', were slower and quieter; the West Germans, or 'Westis', were brasher and more aggressive. The Ossis found the Westis arrogant and rude. The Westis were soon complaining that the Ossis were lazy, shabby and incompetent. On the whole, they did not mix. In 1995, out of over 16,000 weddings celebrated in Berlin, only 562 involved an East Berliner marrying a West Berliner.

At the time of reunification, German chancellor Helmut Kohl painted an optimistic picture of the future. He believed that German free enterprise would create a new 'economic miracle' in Eastern Germany. But the miracle failed to happen. An organization called the Treuhand was set up to sell off factories and businesses that had been owned by the East German state. The East German economy, however, was in a much worse condition than had previously been believed. Many factories were shut because they could not meet Western safety or pollution standards. Some competitors in West Germany bought businesses only in order to close them down.

Renovation work in progress on the Reichstag (parliament) building in Berlin. The new German parliament agreed that the seat of government should be transferred from Bonn to Berlin.

66

## Capitalism's hard lesson

The German novelist Gunter Grass, author of *The Tin Drum*, criticized German reunification. He attacked the way anything good about East Germany was destroyed along with the bad, even health clinics and kindergartens. He also pointed out that, for many East Germans, the harsh effects of free-market economics seemed to confirm what the communists had always said about the capitalist West:

'The citizens of the lost state got to know at close quarters the capitalism which their ideology teachers had once denounced. And lo and behold it hit harder than the most hardline reds had threatened.' (*The Guardian*, 31 May 1997)

99

As more and more money was poured into the effort to revitalize East Germany, disillusion in West Germany mounted. An unpopular 7.5 per cent extra income tax was imposed on Germans to pay for the investment of about 1,000,000,000,000 Deutschmarks in the East. Yet the East German economy failed to revive. Instead, the West German economy also showed signs of strain.

By 1996, an estimated one in four East Germans was unemployed. Even for those in jobs, the experience of reunification was often difficult. In the new Germany, East German job experience and East German

66

## 'What a task we have!'

Many of the new politicians elected to head local government in East German towns and cities struggled with great determination against the problems they faced. One mayor said:

'When citizens have come to me all day with their problems, their loss of jobs, their leaking flats with no toilets, I often lie awake at night worrying. What a task we have! But if we really work hard, I think we'll catch up with the West in about ten years.' (Quoted in Ardagh, *Germany and the Germans*)

99

qualifications often counted for nothing. For example, the civil service was put under the control of West Germans drafted in to transform attitudes and work practices. Many senior people were sacked. Others suffered humiliating 're-education' and downgrading.

Although very few East Germans were nostalgic for communist rule, many soon realized that, in some important details of life, the East had been better for them than the West. For example, mothers in communist East Germany had been able to go out to work because workplaces provided creches to look after their children. Now free creches were closed down and many working mothers had to give up their jobs.

Under German law, all property that had been confiscated by the communist state, or even by the Nazis before that, legally belonged to its original owners or their heirs. This caused much distress – when, for example, people suddenly found that the home they had lived in for decades actually belonged to someone else.

## Facing up to the past

Investigation of the communist past continued to produce shocks. It revealed, for example, that the East German athletes who had won so many Olympic medals had been systematically using performance-enhancing drugs provided by the Stasi. What is more, many top East German sportsmen and women had been Stasi informers. They were in good company.

September 1996: more than 30,000 people protest at cuts in social welfare planned by the German government.

The opening of the Stasi files to the public allowed the identification of many public figures who had been informers, from priests and politicians to novelists and rock musicians. People were allowed to examine their own files, discovering which friends, neighbours or colleagues had passed on information to the Stasi about them. This led to many bitter personal revelations.

66

## Secret files

Under a law passed in 1991, anyone can ask to see the file that was kept on them by the Stasi, the East German secret police. Timothy Garton Ash, a British journalist who read his own 325-page Stasi file, pointed out how terrible the impact of the revelations in a file could be:

'I think of the now famous case of Vera Wollenberg, a political activist ... who discovered from reading her file that her husband, Knud, had been informing on her ever since they met. They would go for a walk with the children on Sunday, and on Monday Knud would be off pouring it all out to his Stasi case officer ... They are now divorced ... Or the writer Hans Joachim Schadlich, who found that his elder brother had been informing on him. And they only discovered from the files. Had the files not been opened, they might still be brother and brother, man and wife ...' (*The File*)

99

The government of the new unified Germany was determined to prosecute those responsible for the deaths on the Berlin Wall, from the leaders such as Erich Honecker, Willy Stoph and Erich Mielke, who gave the orders, down to the border guards who actually pulled the trigger. However, the leaders were mostly old and ill, making a pathetic spectacle. The border guards, mostly young conscripts when they carried out the shootings, argued that they had only been obeying orders. Some were jailed, but without creating any strong sense that justice had been done.

66

## Racism in Berlin

After the collapse of communism, many gangs of East German youths took on extreme racist attitudes. Journalist John Ardagh recounts the experience of one foreign student in Berlin:

'I met a Palestinian student living in West Berlin, who said that after his first brief visit to the East he would never dare to go back: he was shouted at repeatedly, "Go home, you bastard, you're taking our jobs! We'll kill you if you don't get out quick!"' (*Germany and the Germans*)

99

An organized march of neo-Nazis through Dresden, 1991.

## Ugly aftermath

A mixture of bitterness at what they had endured under communism and despair at the mass unemployment that followed reunification made some East Germans turn to political extremism. Neo-Nazi thugs roamed the streets of East Germany, apeing the uniforms and brutality of Adolf Hitler's followers. There were deadly attacks on hostels housing immigrant workers and refugees from former Yugoslavia. Foreigners, accused of taking jobs from East Germans, were an easy target for bottled-up hatreds.

As in many other parts of the former communist bloc, many people in East Germany supported 'reformed' communists. This was not out of a desire to return to the past, but because of a desire for protection against the poverty and insecurity that the sudden introduction of a free market had brought. By 1997, the reformed communist party led by Gregor Gysi had a quarter of the East German vote and more than a third in East Berlin.

The Berlin Wall is now history. It has been demolished and sold off, either in small chunks to tourists or in larger pieces to wealthy individuals or museums. The German parliament has voted to make Berlin the capital of Germany again, and the seat of government, although the changeover from Bonn is taking time.

A West German policeman helps an East German guard through the wall, November 1989.

The Cold War is at an end, and the former communist countries are queuing to join the NATO alliance and the European Union. Yet the brave, bright 'New World Order' dreamed of when communism fell in Eastern Europe remains far off. The scars left by the Iron Curtain still marked both individuals and countries as the end of the millennium approached.

## 66       The Chinese smile

Joachim Meisner, archbishop of Cologne, was interviewed by author David Marsh in 1993. He commented regretfully on how depressed Germans were that the Berlin Wall had come down:

'I really believed that when we had got rid of communism, all our problems would be over. In the Rhineland, they tell the joke: "Why do the Chinese smile? Because they still have the Wall." It is dreadful, dreadful. We should be saying: "Why are we Germans smiling? Because we no longer have the Wall."'
(*Germany and Europe*)

99

# DATE LIST

**1945**

8 May — Germany surrenders after defeat in the Second World War. Soviet troops have control of Berlin.

3 July — By agreement with the Soviets, British, French and US forces occupy their sectors of Berlin – later collectively known as West Berlin.

**1948**

25 February — Soviet-backed communists take a monopoly of power in Czechoslovakia.

24 July — The Soviet forces occupying eastern Germany cut off road and rail routes linking western Germany to West Berlin – the Berlin blockade.

**1949**

4 April — The USA and its West European allies found the North Atlantic Treaty Organization (NATO).

12 May — End of Berlin blockade after the successful Berlin airlift.

23 May — The Federal Republic of Germany (West Germany) is created in the British, French and US zones of occupation.

7 October — The Soviet occupation zone becomes the German Democratic Republic (East Germany), claiming Berlin as its capital.

**1953**

16 June — A workers' uprising begins in East Berlin. It is crushed by Soviet forces.

**1955**

9 May — West Germany joins NATO. In response, the Soviet Union founds the Warsaw Pact in Eastern Europe (14 May).

**1956**

4 November — An uprising against communist rule in Hungary is crushed by Soviet tanks.

**1961**

13 August — The Soviet and East German authorities close the border between East and West Berlin. During the following week, the Berlin Wall is built.

**1962**

17 August — Peter Fechter is shot dead trying to cross the Berlin Wall.

**1963**

26 June — US President John F. Kennedy visits Berlin.

25 December — West Berliners are allowed to cross the wall briefly to meet relatives in East Berlin.

**1968**

20 August — Warsaw Pact forces invade Czechoslovakia, ending the Czechs' attempt to introduce a liberal form of communism

**1971**

31 January — Phone links are restored between East and West Berlin for the first time since the wall was built.

| | |
|---|---|
| 19 March | First ever meeting between the heads of state of East and West Germany, Willy Stoph and Willy Brandt, at Erfurt. |

**1972**

| | |
|---|---|
| 21 December | A Basic Treaty agreed between East and West Germany tries to normalize relations between the two states. |

**1980**

| | |
|---|---|
| 31 August | After widespread strikes led by shipyard electrician Lech Walesa, the Polish communist government agrees to legalize the independent trade union Solidarity. |

**1981**

| | |
|---|---|
| 13 December | Martial law is declared in Poland and many Solidarity leaders are arrested. |

**1985**

| | |
|---|---|
| 11 March | Mikhail Gorbachev becomes First Secretary of the Soviet Communist Party. He advocates major reforms to the communist system. |

**1989**

| | |
|---|---|
| 2 May | The Hungarian government begins to open its border with Austria – the first gap in the Iron Curtain. |
| 12 September | A Solidarity-dominated government takes power in Poland. |
| 7 October | Celebrations to mark the 40th anniversary of the German Democratic Republic, attended by Gorbachev, are the occasion for demonstrations calling for reform. |

| | |
|---|---|
| 18 October | Hardline East German leader Erich Honecker is forced to resign. He is replaced by Egon Krenz. |
| 9 November | The gates in the Berlin Wall are opened and East Berliners are allowed to cross into the West. |
| 6 December | Egon Krenz resigns, marking the end of communist rule in East Germany. |
| 25 December | Romanian communist leader Nicolae Ceausescu and his wife are executed. |
| 29 December | Anti-communist author Vaclav Havel is elected president of Czechoslovakia. |

**1990**

| | |
|---|---|
| 1 July | The West German Deutsch-mark becomes the official currency of East Germany. |
| 3 October | German reunification: East and West Germany are united as a single state. |

**1991**

| | |
|---|---|
| 21 August | An attempted coup by communist hardliners in Moscow is defeated by Russian leader Boris Yeltsin. |
| 25 December | Gorbachev resigns and the Soviet Union ceases to exist. |

**1997**

| | |
|---|---|
| 25 August | Egon Krenz is sentenced to six years in prison for his part in authorizing the killings on the Berlin Wall. |

# GLOSSARY

**capitalism**    term used mostly by socialists and communists to describe the economic system in which people with money invest it in businesses, hoping to make a profit on their investment.

**Cold War**    the armed confrontation between the USA and its allies on one side, and the Soviet Union and its allies on the other, which lasted from the late 1940s to the late 1980s. It was a 'cold war' because the two sides avoided fighting a full-scale military conflict ('hot war').

**communism**    Originally this term was used to describe an ideal state in which private property would have been abolished and all people would be equal. In the twentieth century it has mainly been used for the political and economic system first established in the Soviet Union and spread from there to many other countries, in which a single party ruled without tolerating any opposition, and all industry and agriculture were controlled by the state.

**dissidents**    opponents of the communist regimes in the Soviet Union and Eastern Europe.

**ethnic cleansing**    driving all people of a certain ethnic group out of an area by the use of force and terror.

**free market**    system in which goods and labour are bought and sold for whatever price they will fetch.

**Iron Curtain**    term used for the fortified line dividing Western Europe from communist-controlled Eastern Europe from the late 1940s to 1989.

**NATO**    short for the North Atlantic Treaty Organization: a military alliance set up in 1949 by the USA and its West European allies to oppose the power of the Soviet Union.

**Soviet bloc**    the Soviet Union and those countries around its borders, chiefly in Eastern Europe, that were under Soviet domination.

**Stasi**    the East German secret police, the Staatssicherheitsdienst.

**Soviet Union**    Also known as the Union of Soviet Socialist Republics, or USSR, the Soviet Union was the communist state set up to replace the Russian Empire after the revolution of 1917. It ceased to exist at the end of 1991, when the republics that made up the Soviet Union, including Russia and the Ukraine, became independent states.

**Warsaw Pact**    military alliance set up in 1955 between the Soviet Union and its allies in Eastern Europe – Poland, Czechoslovakia, East Germany, Romania, Bulgaria and Hungary. Albania was also initially a member of the alliance, but withdrew in 1961.

# RESOURCES

## RECOMMENDED READING

Spy novels of the 1960s, such as John Le Carré's *The Spy Who Came in from the Cold* (1963) and Len Deighton's *Funeral in Berlin* (1964) give a feel of Berlin at the period and of the atmosphere of the Cold War. There are films of these books, and of other spy stories of the time, that you might catch on television: for example, Hitchcock's movie *The Torn Curtain*, which is set in East Germany.

Other novels you could read are:
 Ian McEwan's macabre *The Black Dogs*, which is set in Berlin in the 1950s;
Malcolm Bradbury's *Rates of Exchange*, a satire on life in communist Eastern Europe;
Saul Bellow's *The Dean's December*, a serious novel that includes a powerful ironic portrait of life in Romania under the Ceausescu dictatorship.

*Football against the Enemy*, by Simon Kuper, looks at the relationship between soccer and politics across the world. The sections on East Germany and the Soviet Union tell much about how those societies worked. *Stalin's Nose* by Rory Maclean (Flamingo, 1993) is an amusing series of surreal snapshots of life in Eastern Europe before and after the Berlin Wall. For more depth, try *The File* by Timothy Garton Ash. This centres on his painful experience of reading his own Stasi file.

## FILMS

The weird films of Kryzsztof Kiesolowski (e.g. *Three Colours: White*) show Poland since the fall of communism. Many films by the great Polish director Andrzej Wajda, such as *Man of Marble*, show communism in action.

## SOURCES

Sources of information for this book were:
John Ardagh, *Germany and the Germans*, Penguin, 1995
Timothy Garton Ash, *The File: A Personal History*, HarperCollins, 1997
Timothy Garton Ash, *The Uses of Adversity*, Granta Books, 1989
Willy Brandt, *People and Politics*, Collins, 1978
Gordon A. Craig, *The Germans*, Penguin, 1982
Fulbrook, *Anatomy of a Dictatorship*
Cornelia Heins, *The Wall Falls*, Grey Seal, 1994
Simon Kuper, *Football Against the Enemy*, Phoenix, 1994
David Marsh, *Germany and Europe: The Crisis of Unity*, Mandarin, 1995
A. James McAdams, *Germany Divided: From the Wall to Reunification*, Princeton University, 1993
Ken Smith, *Berlin, Coming in from the Cold*, Penguin, 1990
Ann Tusa, *The Last Division: Berlin and the Wall*, Hodder and Stoughton, 1996

# INDEX

Adenauer, Konrad **19**
Allied Control Council **13**
Austria **39, 40**

Berlin blockade **16, 17, 18**
Berlin uprising **20**
Bernauerstrasse **9, 29**
Blake, George **22**
Bolsheviks **12**
border guards **23, 26, 28, 43, 56**

Brandenburg Gate **3, 7, 8, 20, 27**
Brandt, Willy **11, 26, 27, 30**
Brecht, Bertolt **21**
Brezhnev, Leonid **31, 38**
Britain **5, 11, 13, 16, 47, 49**
Bulgaria **14**

capitalism **12, 37, 47, 48**
checkpoints **9, 26, 31**
Checkpoint Charlie **26**

churches **32, 41**
Churchill, Winston **5, 12, 14**
Cold War **4, 10, 24, 25, 27, 30, 37, 58**
communism **12, 14, 15, 33, 37, 38, 45, 47, 48, 50, 52, 55**
Communist Party **12, 13, 14, 51**
Czechoslovakia **14, 34, 35, 39, 40, 45, 53**

Democratic Socialist Party  **46**
Deutschmark  **16, 45, 48, 49, 54**
dissidents  **35**
Dubcek, Alexander  **35**

East Germany, *see* German Democratic Republic

Fechter, Peter  **28**
Federal Republic of Germany (FRG)  **5, 19, 49**
France  **5, 13, 16, 47, 49**
Free German Youth  **34**
Fulbright, William  **25**

German Democratic Republic (GDR)  **4, 6, 19, 41**
Gerlach, Manfred  **41, 46**
glasnost  **37**
Gorbachev, Mikhail  **37, 41, 42, 50, 51**
Grepos  **7**
Gysi, Gregor  **46, 58**

Havel, Vaclev  **45**
Heym, Stefan  **15, 42**
Honecker, Erich  **30, 31, 40, 41, 42, 43, 56**
Hungarian uprising  **20, 21**
Hungary  **14, 20, 21, 38, 39, 40**

Iron Curtain  **4, 14, 23, 39**

Jaruzelski, Wojciech  **36**
Jews  **15**

Kennedy, John F.  **24, 25, 26, 27**
Khrushchev, Nikita  **24, 25, 27, 37**
Kohl, Helmut  **47, 49, 52, 53**
Krenz, Egon  **43, 46**

Liftin, Gunter  **9**

Marshall Plan  **15**

Nazis  **11, 15, 18, 55, 57**
Neues Forum  **40, 41, 42, 43, 48, 49**
nuclear war  **22, 25**

Olympic Games  **32, 55**
Ostmarks  **49**

perestroika  **37**
Poland  **14, 36, 38, 40**
Pope John Paul II  **36**
Prague Spring  **34, 35**

Reichstag  **13, 53**
reunification  **47, 48, 49, 50, 51, 53, 54, 57**
Reuter, Ernst  **16, 18**
Romania  **14, 45**
Roosevelt, Franklin D.  **5**

Sinatra Doctrine  **38**
socialism  **12, 15, 31, 37, 48**
Socialist Unity Party  **31, 33, 46**

Solidarity  **36, 38**
Soviet bloc  **4, 12, 30, 36, 37, 40**
Soviet Union  **4, 5, 6, 11, 12, 13, 14, 16, 19, 24, 25, 30, 35, 37, 38, 41, 47, 49, 50, 51, 52**
spies  **22**
Stalin, Josef  **5, 13**
Stasi  **7, 15, 19, 22, 34, 35, 40, 41, 46, 55, 56**
Stoph, Willy  **6, 31, 56**

Teltow Canal  **8, 9**
Treuhand  **53**
Truman, Harry S.  **14, 15**

Ulbricht, Walter  **19, 24, 30**
United Nations  **30**
USA  **4, 5, 11, 13, 14, 15, 16, 25, 47, 49**

Vopos  **5, 6, 7, 8, 23**

Walesa, Lech  **36, 38, 39**
War, Second World  **4, 5, 11, 14, 49**
West Germany, *see* Federal Republic of Germany
Wolf, Markus  **41**

Yalta Conference  **5**
Yeltsin, Boris  **51**
Yugoslavia  **52, 57**